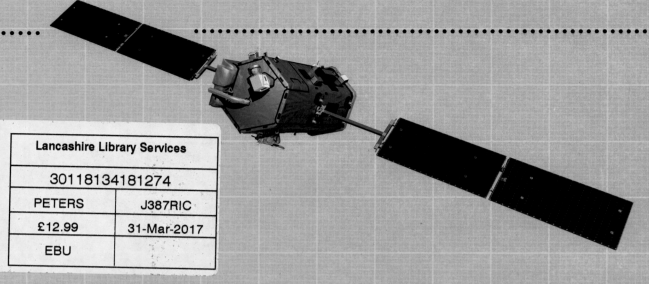

Franklin Watts
First published in Great Britain in 2016 by
The Watts Publishing Group

Credits
Conceived, designed and edited by
Tall Tree Ltd
Series Editor: David John
Series Designer: Jonathan Vipond

ISBN 978 1 4451 5026 0

Printed in China

Franklin Watts
An imprint of
Hachette Children's Group
Part of The Watts Publishing Group
Carmelite House
50 Victoria Embankment
London EC4Y 0DZ

An Hachette UK Company
www.hachette.co.uk

www.franklinwatts.co.uk

Picture credits:
t-top, b-bottom, l-left, r-right, c-centre
All images public domain unless
otherwise indicated:
Front cover c all courtesy of NASA, front cover
bcl., 5cr Dreamstime.com/Helgidinson, front
cover bcr 3t, 5l Dreamstime.com/Mikephotos,
3b, Back cover all courtesy of NASA,
1, 17br Dreamstime.com/James Steidl, 2t, 4,
14–15 all, 16 all, 16-17c , 18-23 all, 24bl, 25
both, 26-27 all, 28-29 all, 31r courtesy of
NASA, 17tr Dreamstime.com/Siberian180762

CONTENTS

4 FLYING THROUGH SPACE

6 FLOATING INTO SPACE

8 EARLY ROCKETS

10 USING ROCKETS

12 THE SPACE RACE

14 RACE TO THE MOON

16 SPACECRAFT DESIGN

18 SATELLITES

20 TELESCOPES IN SPACE

22 EXPLORING THE SOLAR SYSTEM

24 SPACE ROVERS

26 LIVING IN SPACE

28 BOMBS AND SAILS

30 GLOSSARY

32 INDEX

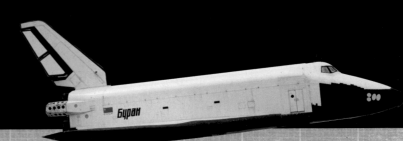

FLYING THROUGH SPACE

The idea of leaving Earth to explore the Universe has fascinated people for centuries. However, it's only been in the last seventy years that we've been able to send spacecraft out into space.

INTO SPACE ☞

Since the first space flights of the 1950s, we've sent missions to explore every planet in the Solar System, as well as its moons, the Sun and even comets. However, the only body beyond Earth that humans have set foot on is the Moon. Between 1969 and 1972, 12 people walked on the Moon, and that took some serious science!

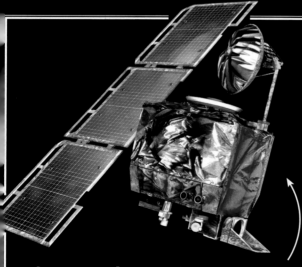

Sent to study Mars in 1998, the Mars Climate Orbiter crashed into the red planet. A mix-up between imperial and metric measurements meant that its trajectory was wrong.

IT IS ROCKET SCIENCE!

Getting into space requires a huge amount of energy (more of that later), and trying to reach another planet requires some incredibly complicated maths. Imagine trying to hit an object that's millions of kilometres away and moving at thousands of kilometres an hour, while you're moving at thousands of kilometres an hour yourself! It's not surprising that things sometimes go wrong.

GET HOME SAFELY

Even if astronauts reach their target, getting home from space is no easy matter. The atmosphere, a blanket of gases surrounding Earth, can make things a little hot for incoming astronauts. Friction from the atmosphere causes temperatures of up to 1,650°C during re-entry. Spacecraft need special heat shields to protect any passengers and crew.

The USA uses non-reusable rockets, such as this Delta II, to launch its spacecraft.

The heat shield of the Apollo 10 command module protected the crew during re-entry.

A COMMON SIGHT?

These days, space flights are fairly common. There were more than 85 space launches in 2015 alone. Russia, the USA and China accounted for more than 80 per cent of these launches. Other space agencies include India's and private companies such as SpaceX.

FLOATING INTO SPACE

In the past, writers, artists and scientists thought of many ways of reaching space. While most would never get off the ground, some were close to modern space flight.

SUNLIGHT AND DEW ☞

The 17th-century French writer Cyrano de Bergerac dreamed up many ingenious, though impossible, ways of getting into space. These included strapping on bottles of morning dew which, when heated by the Sun, drew him into the air. However, de Bergerac also described how rockets could be used to power a craft through space.

De Bergerac's hero, covered in dew bottles, floats into the air.

☜ FIRED FROM A GUN

In his 1865 novel, *From the Earth to the Moon*, French writer Jules Verne tells the story of a group of gun club members who build an enormous cannon to blast a capsule towards the Moon. While such a device would be possible in theory, the acceleration created would kill anyone inside the capsule!

The science fiction writer Jules Verne.

In this illustration from From the Earth to the Moon, *the astronauts enter the capsule.*

FIRED FROM A GUN... AGAIN! ☞

In 1902, French film-maker Georges Méliès made *A Trip to the Moon*, based on Verne's novel. The movie shows a team of scientists travelling to the Moon in a capsule fired from a gun. They explore the Moon's surface, escape from lunar aliens and return to a hero's welcome back on Earth.

ANTI GRAVITY

In his 1901 novel The First Men in the Moon, *English writer H G Wells wrote about a fictional material called cavorite, a substance able to counter the force of gravity. He tells the story of a scientist who covers a capsule in cavorite and floats up to the Moon.*

EARLY ROCKETS

The earliest rockets were used for entertainment and warfare. However, a few enterprising individuals saw their possibility for transport, sometimes with disastrous results.

The first recorded use of rockets in battle was in 1232, when Chinese soldiers fired them at attacking Mongol forces.

CHINESE ROCKETS

No one is sure when the first rockets were built, but the Chinese have been using them for hundreds of years. Chinese engineers packed a solid fuel – gunpowder – into pointed tubes and fired them at enemy troops.

Wan Hu on his rocket chair.

THE FIRST ASTRONAUT?

Legend tells of a Chinese official known as Wan Hu who thought it might be a good idea to strap 47 rockets to a chair to see if he could fly. The attempt ended in disaster, when both rockets and chair exploded. In memory of his experiment, Wan Hu now has a crater on the Moon named after him.

Konstantin Tsiolkovsky

👉 SPACE IDEAS

In 1903, Russian scientist Konstantin Tsiolkovsky published some quite accurate theories about travelling through space. One of these involved the use of liquid-fuel rockets, which hadn't been invented yet. That task fell to American engineer and inventor Robert Goddard. In March 1926, he launched the world's first liquid-fuel rocket, which flew up to a height of 12 metres and travelled 56 metres before landing in a cabbage patch.

Goddard, shown with the first liquid-fuel rocket, also came up with the idea of using multi-stage rockets, a key idea for getting into space.

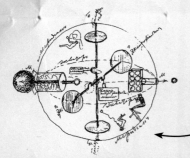

One of Tsiolkovsky's less viable ideas is this sketch for a space station.

LIQUID-FUEL ROCKETS

Unlike solid-fuel rockets, which use granules or pellets containing both the fuel and the oxidiser mixed together, liquid-fuel rockets use both a fuel and an oxidiser in liquid form. These are pumped into a combustion chamber where the oxidiser helps the fuel to burn. This creates a blast of hot gases, which roar out of the nozzle, pushing the rocket forwards.

Blast of gases

Nozzle

Combustion chamber

Oxidiser tank

Fuel tank

USING ROCKETS

As rockets became more powerful in the first half of the 20th century, people started to use them to drive a range of vehicles, as well as powerful, long-range weapons.

ROCKET VEHICLES

In the late 1920s, German car maker Opel built a series of solid-fuel rocket vehicles, including cars, an aircraft and a train. One of the cars roared to a speed of 230 km/h, while one of the rocket trains blasted to 290 km/h before it leapt off the tracks and was destroyed. The glider flew for just 75 seconds, covering 1.5 km before it crashed and was destroyed.

Opel's rocket car had upside-down wings to prevent it lifting up into the air at great speeds.

Opel's rocket train races along a track in 1928.

ROCKET WEAPON

During the Second World War (1939–1945), German scientists developed the world's first long-range ballistic missile, the V-2 rocket. From 1944, some 3,000 V-2s were fired at London, England, and Antwerp, Belgium. After the war, German scientists were taken to the USA and the Soviet Union to start work on those countries' space programmes.

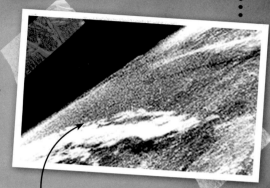

The first picture of the Earth from space was taken by a camera on a V-2 rocket launched by the US in October 1946.

In 1950, the US launches Bumper 8, based on the V-2, to study rocket technology.

WERNHER VON BRAUN

Leading the team that designed the V-2 was German rocket scientist Wernher von Braun. As the war came to an end, with Germany losing, von Braun and some of his team decided to surrender to US troops. They were taken to the USA, where they continued working on V-2s and developing other rockets. Von Braun went on to create the huge Saturn V rockets, which blasted astronauts towards the Moon (see pp. 14–15).

Von Braun (centre with a broken arm) surrenders to US troops in May 1945.

THE SPACE RACE

After the end of the Second World War, the Soviet Union and the USA started to compete with each other to see who could record notable firsts in space exploration.

Sputnik 1

👉 SPUTNIK

Using the German V-2 rocket as a starting point, both sides in the space race developed their own launchers. On 4 October 1957, a Soviet R7 rocket blasted the small *Sputnik 1* satellite into space, making it the first man-made object to orbit (go round) Earth.

SPACE PIONEERS

The first living things sent into space were fruit flies on board a V-2 rocket launched from New Mexico, USA, in 1947. The flies were parachuted back to Earth alive, unlike the first mammal to orbit Earth. On 3 November 1957, the dog Laika was launched inside the Soviet spacecraft Sputnik 2. *She died during the mission.*

👉 US FAILURE

Shocked by the Soviet success with *Sputnik 1*, the US decided to pull forward the launch of its first satellite. On 6 December 1957, on live TV, the Vanguard rocket reached a height of one metre before falling back and exploding! The following year, the US formed the National Aeronautics and Space Administration (NASA).

The Vanguard rocket explodes on the launchpad.

FIRST PEOPLE

The Soviet Union went on to record other firsts in space exploration, including sending the first man, Yuri Gagarin, into space in 1961, and the first woman, Valentina Tereshkova, in 1963. In an attempt to catch up, the US turned its attention to reaching the Moon first.

Yuri Gagarin

Valentina Tereshkova

RACE TO THE MOON

With the focus now on reaching the Moon, the race was on to see whether the Soviet Union or the USA would be the first to plant their flag on the lunar surface.

SOVIET FAILURE

This time, it was the Soviets' turn to experience failure. Their secret Moon programme was meant to use the powerful N1 rockets. But problems and failures with a number of launches meant that they weren't able to get their programme off the ground.

Soyuz spacecraft, which formed the basis of the Soviet Moon missions, are still used today to carry people and supplies to the International Space Station (see p.19).

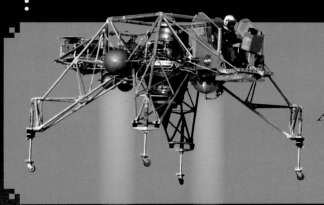

TESTING TIMES

This bizarre aircraft was used to train NASA's Apollo pilots, allowing them to practise landing on the Moon's surface. During one such test flight, astronaut Neil Armstrong got into trouble and had to blast free using his ejector seat.

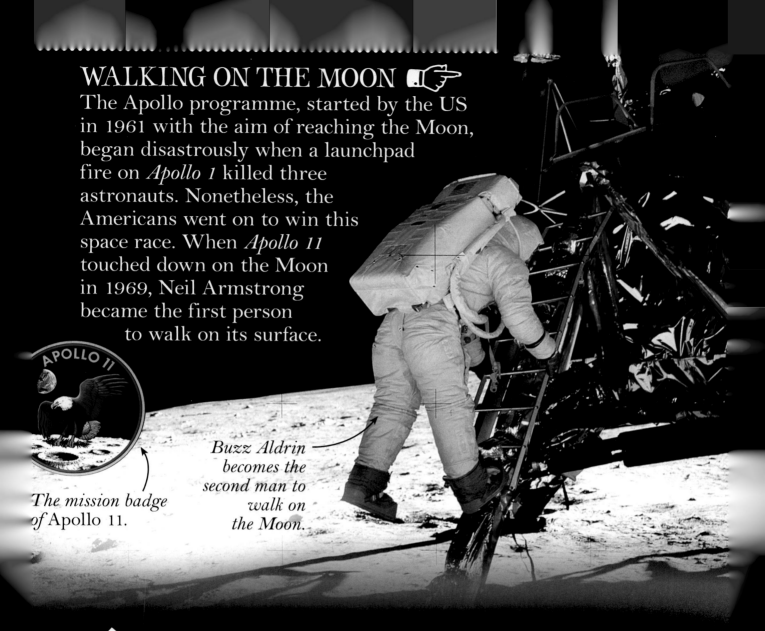

WALKING ON THE MOON ☞

The Apollo programme, started by the US in 1961 with the aim of reaching the Moon, began disastrously when a launchpad fire on *Apollo 1* killed three astronauts. Nonetheless, the Americans went on to win this space race. When *Apollo 11* touched down on the Moon in 1969, Neil Armstrong became the first person to walk on its surface.

The mission badge of Apollo 11.

Buzz Aldrin becomes the second man to walk on the Moon.

The Apollo 13 *astronauts 'splashdown' safely.*

APOLLO 13

Despite the success of Apollo 11, *the US Apollo programme did not proceed without problems. Apollo 13 experienced an explosion during its mission. For five tense and dramatic days, the crew had to nurse their spacecraft around the Moon and back to Earth, before returning safely on 17 April 1970.*

SPACECRAFT
DESIGN

Soyuz and Apollo were single-use spacecraft. The next development was to design a spacecraft that could be used for many missions.

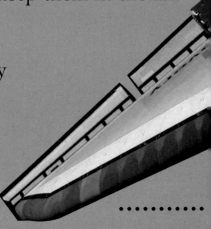

The US's M2-F2 was a wingless, rocket-powered aircraft.

The US's X-24A experimental aircraft was carried under a B-52 bomber before being released and firing its rocket engines. It could glide back to Earth.

LIFTING BODIES

The USA and the Soviet Union wanted to create a spacecraft that could be piloted back to Earth and land on a runway, just like a plane. To test possible designs, NASA built various lifting body aircraft. These have small or no wings and rely on the shape of their body to create the lift needed to keep them in the air.

REUSABLE SPACECRAFT

The result of NASA's experiments with lifting body aircraft was the Space Transportation System, or Space Shuttle. The Shuttle fleet went into space on a total of 135 missions between 1981 and 2011. They landed like planes, and could be reused.

SNOWSTORM

Looking very much like the Space Shuttle, the Soviet Union's reusable spacecraft was called Buran, *meaning 'Snowstorm'. However, it made only one unmanned orbital flight in 1988. The project was cancelled in 1993 after the collapse of the Soviet Union.*

The Soviet Buran orbiter

The US Space Shuttle carried its payload in a large cargo hold on its back.

SPACESHIPONE

SpaceShipOne, *built by Mojave Aerospace Ventures, became the first spacecraft to complete a manned, private spaceflight in 2004. It was carried into the air by a mother aircraft, before firing its rocket engine to blast to a height of 100 km (the official boundary between the atmosphere and space). It then glided back down to Earth.*

SpaceShipOne *won the $10 million Ansari X prize by making two flights into space.*

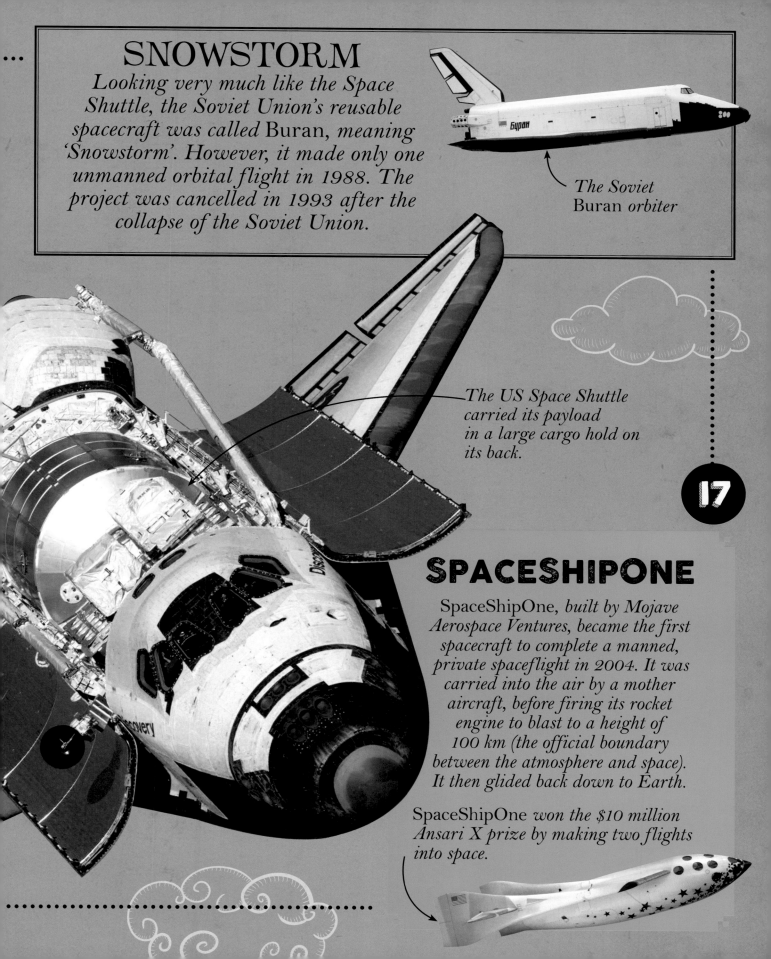

SATELLITES

After the success of Sputnik (see p.12), scientists realised that satellites could have many useful benefits. They could be used to see what weather was heading our way, bounce phone and TV signals around the world and even spy on other countries.

The Orbiting Carbon Observatory satellite studies Earth's atmosphere.

STUDYING EARTH

Over the years, hundreds of satellites have been launched into orbit around Earth. They perform a wide range of tasks. Some take detailed pictures of the planet's surface, while others collect scientific data. Some form part of the Global Positioning System (GPS) and can be used to pinpoint locations on Earth.

☞ LAUNCH FAILURE

Sometimes launches go wrong. In 2014, the rocket carrying Cygnus CRS ORb-3, taking cargo to the International Space Station, blew up after launch. Improving engines and better pre-launch checks will make rockets more reliable.

LACK OF GLORY ☞

NASA's *Glory* satellite was designed to study Earth's atmosphere. However, when it launched in 2011, the nose cone housing the satellite failed to open properly, so the satellite fell back to Earth and burnt up in the atmosphere.

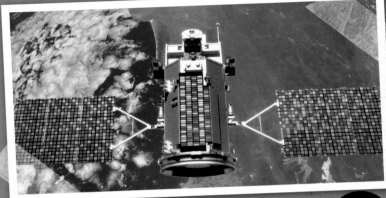

19

TYPES OF ORBIT

The International Space Station is a habitable satellite in a low Earth orbit, 330–435 km above Earth's surface (see p.27). GPS satellites are found in a medium Earth orbit (2,000–35,000 km), while geosynchronous satellites (which stay above one place on Earth's surface) are found 35,786 km above Earth's surface.

Medium Earth

Low Earth

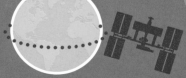

Geosynchronous

TELESCOPES IN SPACE

Space is a great place from which to look at the stars. With no atmosphere in the way to cloud the picture, you can get pin-sharp views of the cosmos – providing your equipment has been put together properly.

Hubble image of a star-forming nebula.

EYE IN THE SKY

In 1990, the Hubble Space Telescope was put into orbit to study the Universe. However, it soon became obvious there was something wrong – the pictures it was sending back were not very sharp. There was a problem with the telescope's huge mirror. It had been made to exacting standards, but it was the wrong shape!

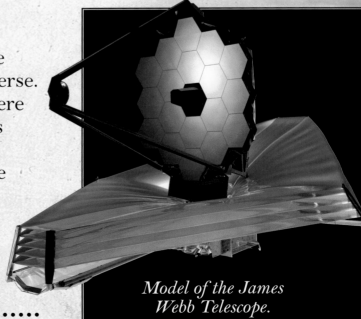

Model of the James Webb Telescope.

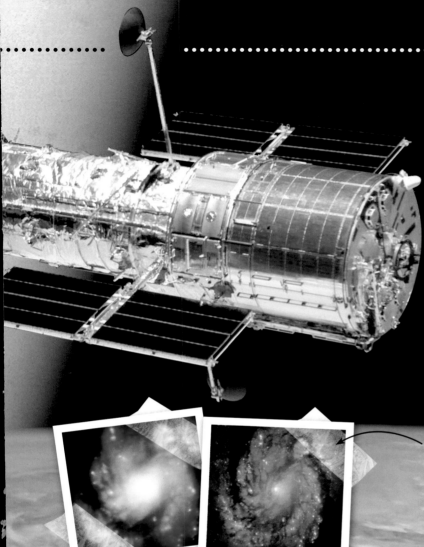

☛ CORRECTING BLURRED VISION

It would have been too expensive to bring Hubble back down to Earth to fix it, so NASA developed equipment that would act as 'spectacles' and correct the blurred vision. After a service mission, the equipment was fitted and Hubble started to send back amazing images of the Universe.

The improvement in Hubble's vision allowed it to take clearer images with more vivid colours, as seen in these pictures of the same galaxy taken before (left) and after (right) Hubble's repair.

BIGGER AND BETTER

While Hubble may continue to operate until 2040, space agencies are already building bigger and better telescopes to put into orbit. One of these is the NASA-designed James Webb Space Telescope. This odd-looking spacecraft will have a segmented mirror measuring 6.5 m across to provide astonishing image resolution.

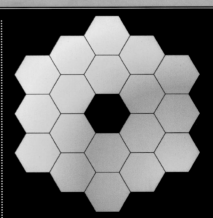

Hubble primary mirror

James Webb Space Telescope primary mirror

DIAMETER

2.4m   6.5 m

EXPLORING THE SOLAR SYSTEM

Space is a harsh place to explore. Crossing millions of kilometres of a freezing vacuum is bad enough, but things can get even worse when you reach your destination.

Image of the surface of Venus taken by a Venera probe in 1975.

☞ SURVIVAL!

Space probes have to be tough enough to survive a long journey and the extreme conditions they might face on a planet's surface. The Soviet Venera probes that reached the surface of Venus between 1961 and 1984 recorded temperatures of more than 450°C and winds of up to 325 km/h.

VISITING THE OUTER PLANETS ☞

Perhaps the most successful exploration missions involved the two US Voyager probes. Launched in 1977, *Voyager 1* and *Voyager 2* were sent to study the outer planets of Jupiter, Saturn, Uranus and Neptune. Having flown past the planets, the two probes are still flying out of the Solar System and towards the stars.

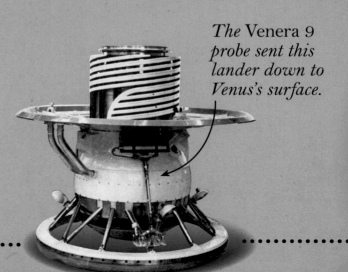

The Venera 9 *probe sent this lander down to Venus's surface.*

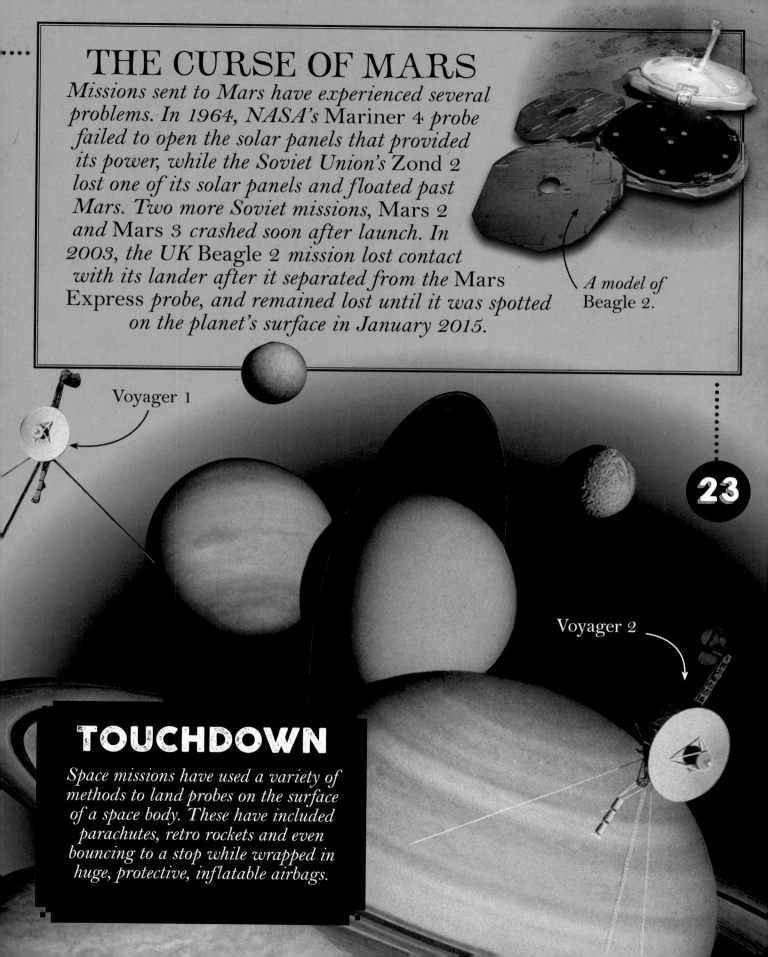

THE CURSE OF MARS

Missions sent to Mars have experienced several problems. In 1964, NASA's Mariner 4 probe failed to open the solar panels that provided its power, while the Soviet Union's Zond 2 lost one of its solar panels and floated past Mars. Two more Soviet missions, Mars 2 and Mars 3 crashed soon after launch. In 2003, the UK Beagle 2 mission lost contact with its lander after it separated from the Mars Express probe, and remained lost until it was spotted on the planet's surface in January 2015.

A model of Beagle 2.

Voyager 1

Voyager 2

TOUCHDOWN

Space missions have used a variety of methods to land probes on the surface of a space body. These have included parachutes, retro rockets and even bouncing to a stop while wrapped in huge, protective, inflatable airbags.

SPACE ROVERS

Roving vehicles allow scientists to study and explore much more of a planet's surface than would be possible with a static lander.

LUNOKHOD

The first Lunokhod, a Soviet robot vehicle, was destroyed during its launch in 1969 when the rocket carrying it blew up. The second Lunokhod, confusingly called *Lunokhod 1*, landed on the Moon in November 1970. It operated for 322 days and covered 10.5 km, sending photographs and surface data back to Earth. *Lunokhod 2* landed in January 1973. It worked for about four months.

A model of Lunokhod 2, *which explored 40 km of the Moon's surface.*

APOLLO LUNAR ROVING VEHICLE

The Lunar Roving Vehicle was designed to carry astronauts around the Moon during the last three Apollo missions. Each wheel had its own electric motor and a 'tyre' made out of a wire mesh to save weight.

US astronaut Eugene Cernan driving the lunar rover during the Apollo 17 *mission.*

MARS ROVERS

NASA has sent four robot rovers to Mars. The first, the tiny, slow-moving Sojourner, *landed in 1997 and covered just 0.1 km. Next were twin rovers,* Spirit *(2003) and* Opportunity *(2005).* Spirit *operated for more than six years, but only covered 7.7 km because its wheels became stuck.* Opportunity *is still active, and has covered more than 40 km of the surface. The latest rover is* Curiosity, *which landed in 2012. Its mission is to study Martian climate and geology.*

Opportunity *took this image of a rock spire in the Spirit of St. Louis Crater.*

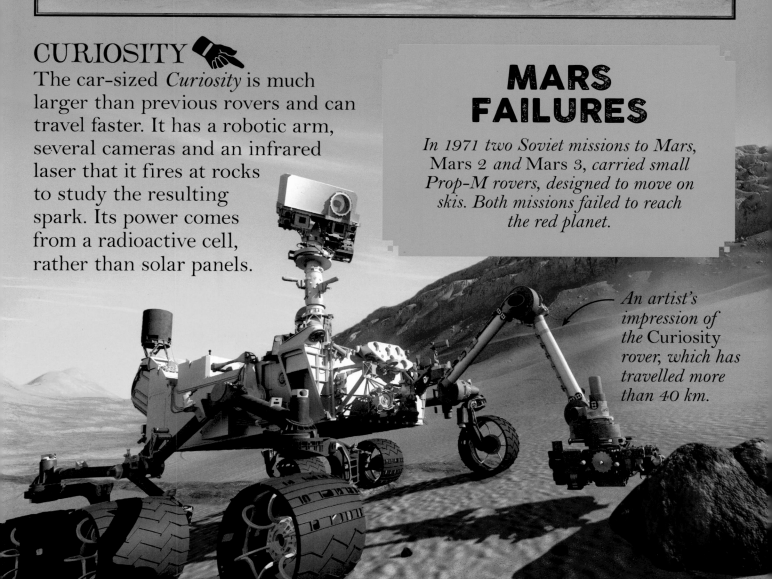

CURIOSITY

The car-sized *Curiosity* is much larger than previous rovers and can travel faster. It has a robotic arm, several cameras and an infrared laser that it fires at rocks to study the resulting spark. Its power comes from a radioactive cell, rather than solar panels.

MARS FAILURES

In 1971 two Soviet missions to Mars, Mars 2 and Mars 3, carried small Prop-M rovers, designed to move on skis. Both missions failed to reach the red planet.

An artist's impression of the Curiosity *rover, which has travelled more than 40 km.*

LIVING IN SPACE

Solar panels

Since the 1970s, the Soviet Union and the USA have built a number of space stations to study the effects of living in space for long periods of time.

SALYUT

The first series of stations was Salyut. Despite two failures, the Soviet Union succeeded in putting four Salyut space stations into orbit. From 1971 to 1986, these craft were used for scientific studies, as well as secret military experiments.

SKYLAB 👉

The USA's answer to Salyut was Skylab, which met with problems as soon as it was launched in 1973. A protective shield was torn away and the solar panel became jammed. The station was overheating and couldn't generate enough power. In a rescue mission, astronauts deployed a sunshade to cool things down and free the panel. Skylab remained in orbit until 1979.

Skylab is shown here with its solar panels in the correct position. The makeshift sunshade is draped over the main body of the space station.

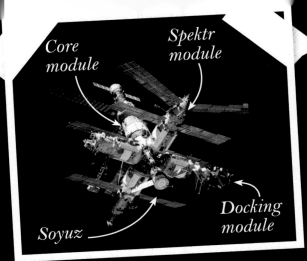

Core module

Spektr module

Soyuz

Docking module

This image of the space station Mir, taken by a visiting crew member, shows its different modules.

☞ MIR

Mir, a modular Soviet space station, was launched in 1986 and assembled from various parts, or modules, in orbit. The station had a number of accidents, including computer failures, power loss, fires and even crashes with visiting spacecraft! It was in use until 2001.

☞ INTERNATIONAL SPACE STATION

A joint project by five space agencies, including Russia's and NASA, the International Space Station (ISS) was launched in 1998. With more than 4,000 square metres of solar panels, it is the size of a football pitch. It orbits Earth once every 92 minutes.

The ISS can accommodate up to six astronauts at a time.

BOMBS AND SAILS

While the only way to get into space today is by using a fuel-burning rocket, scientists have been looking at other methods of propelling spacecraft through the cosmos.

ION DRIVE 👉

Moving through space on a jet of ionised gas sounds like science fiction, but it's actually science fact. An ion thruster produces a jet of charged particles called ions and as these fly out of the back of a spacecraft, they push the spacecraft forwards. Ion thrusters have been fitted to several spacecraft, including NASA's *Deep Space* 1 in 1998, and the European Space Agency's LISA *Pathfinder* in 2015.

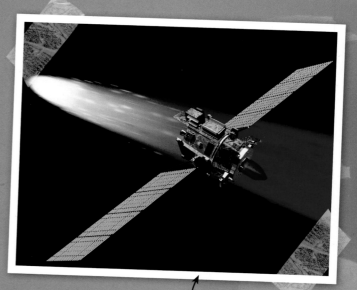

Deep Space 1 *shown using its ion thruster to approach a comet.*

Launched in 1964, SERT-1 was the first spacecraft to be powered by an ion thruster.

SAILING THROUGH SPACE

Radiation from the Sun produces pressure on any spacecraft. Scientists believed they could use this radiation pressure to travel to planets in the Solar System using huge, ultra-thin mirrors as 'sails'. They were proved right in May 2010, when the Japanese probe *IKAROS* was launched. It reached Venus six months later, becoming the first solar sail to travel between planets.

NASA launched its first sail-powered spacecraft, the NanoSail-D2 in November 2010.

NUCLEAR POWER

One of the earliest ideas for space propulsion involved nuclear explosions! Project Orion was started by the US in 1958 and proposed releasing small atomic bombs behind a spacecraft. As the bombs exploded, they would push against the spacecraft, thrusting it through space. Luckily, the idea of exploding powerful bombs near spacecraft never got off the ground!

Artist's impression of an atomic bomb-powered spacecraft.

GLOSSARY

ATMOSPHERE
The layer of gases and clouds that surrounds a star, planet or moon. Earth's atmosphere is called air.

COMBUSTION CHAMBER
A chamber in a combustion engine, such as on a jet or a rocket, in which a mix of fuel and air is burned. In a jet or rocket, this produces a blast of hot gases which pushes the vehicle forwards.

FRICTION
The resistance that a surface encounters when moving over another surface or through a liquid or gas. High levels of friction make it harder for objects to move.

GPS
Short for Global Positioning System, this uses a network of satellites to allow people to pinpoint their position on Earth.

GRAVITY
The attractive force with which every object pulls on every other object.

IMPERIAL UNIT
A unit of the imperial measurement system. Imperial units include a mile, a yard, an inch, a foot and a pound.

LIFTING BODY
A specially shaped aircraft which uses the shape of its body rather than wings to produce the lift needed to keep it in the air.

METRIC UNIT
A unit of the metric system, an international system of standard decimal measurement. Metric units include a metre, a centimetre and kilogramme.

NASA
The National Aeronautics and Space Administration, the organisation responsible for the United States' civilian space programme. It was set up by the US government in 1958.

NEBULA
A huge cloud of gas and dust lying out in space. Many nebulas glow and are brightly coloured, while others absorb light and appear black.

ORBIT
A path taken by one object around another object, such as the orbit of a moon around a planet.

OXIDISER
Something that chemically binds fuel with oxygen so that the fuel can burn, such as in a jet or a rocket engine.

PAYLOAD
The carrying capacity of a launch vehicle, which can be equipment, cargo, passengers, or crew, usually measured in terms of weight.

PROBE
A robotic, unmanned spacecraft.

PROPULSION
The act of thrusting forwards. In rocket science, jet propulsion is thrust produced by passing a jet of matter in the opposite direction from the direction of motion.

RADIATION
Energetic particles that are given off by objects, such as visible light that is emitted by a star.

RETRO ROCKET
A rocket engine that provides thrust to oppose the motion of a vehicle, and cause it to slow down.

SATELLITE
In spaceflight, an artificial satellite that has been put into orbit. The term is also used to describe natural satellites, such as moons.

SOVIET UNION
The Communist state that existed in Russia and its allied republics between 1922 and 1991.

SPLASHDOWN
Returning to Earth from a space mission and landing in the sea, with a splash.

TRAJECTORY
The path followed by a flying object.

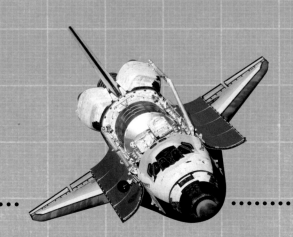

INDEX

Aldrin, Buzz 15
Ansar X prize 17
Apollo programme
    14–15, 16
Apollo 1 15
Apollo 10 5
Apollo 11 15
Apollo 13 15
Armstrong, Neil 14, 15
atmosphere 5
atomic bombs 29

B-52 16
Beagle 2 23
Bumper 8 11
Buran 17

Chinese rockets 8
combustion 9
comets 4, 28
Curiosity 25
Cygnus CRS ORb-3

de Bergerac, Cyrano, 6
Deep Space 1 28
Delta II 5

Gagarin, Yuri 13
geosynchronous satellites
    19
glider 10
Glory 19
Goddard, Robert 9
GPS 18
gunpowder 8

heat shield 5
Hubble Space Telescope
    20–21

IKAROS 29
International Space
    Station 14, 19, 27
ion drive 28

James Webb Space
    Telescope 21

Laika 12
liquid-fuel rockets 9
LISA Pathfinder 28
Lunar Roving Vehicle 24
Lunokhod 24

M2-F2 16
Mariner 4 23
Mars 4, 23, 25
Mars Climate Orbiter 4
Mars Express 23
Méliès, Georges 7
Mir 27
Moon 4, 7, 8, 11, 13,
    14–15, 24

N1 rockets 14
NanoSail-D2 29
NASA 13, 16, 19, 21, 23,
    25
nebula 20

Observatory 18
Opel 10
Opportunity 25
Orbiting Carbon Orion
    (Project) 29
oxidiser 9

Prop-M rovers 25

rovers 24

sailing (space) 29
Salyut 26
satellites 18–19
Saturn V 11
Second World War 11
SERT-1 28
Skylab 26
Sojourner 25
Solar System 4
solid fuel 8, 10
Soyuz 14, 16
SpaceShipOne 17
Space Shuttle 16, 17
space stations 9, 26–27
Spirit 25
Sputnik 1 12, 13
Sputnik 2 12

telescopes 20–21
Tereshkova, Valentina 13
train (rocket) 10
Tsiolkovsky, Konstantin 9

V-2 rockets 11, 12
Venera probes 22
Vanguard rocket 13
Venus 22, 29
Verne, Jules 7
von Braun 11
Voyager probes 22-23

warfare 8
Wan Hu 8
Wells, H G 7

X-24A 16

Zond 2 23

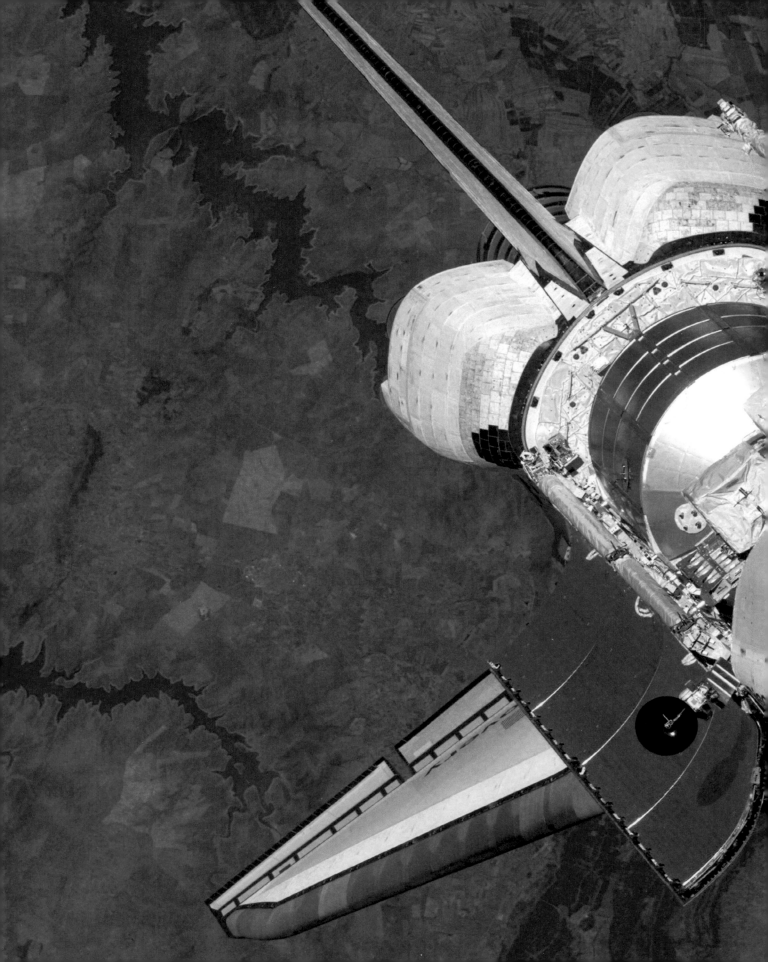